香港國際詩歌之夜 2019
INTERNATIONAL POETRY NIGHTS IN HONG KONG

主辦單位 Organizer

香港詩歌節基金會

Hong Kong Poetry Festival Foundation

編輯 Editors

宋子江 Chris Song

柯夏智 Lucas Klein

陳嘉恩 Shelby K. Y. Chan

傍晚在鰂魚涌

鍾國強

DUSK AT QUARRY BAY

DEREK CHUNG

《傍晚在鰂魚涌》
鍾國強 著

封面影像：北島
封面設計：麥安

國際統一書號（ISBN）：978-988-237-148-4

出版：香港中文大學出版社
香港 新界 沙田・香港中文大學
傳真：+852 2603 7355
電郵：cup@cuhk.edu.hk
網址：www.chineseupress.com

Dusk at Quarry Bay
By Derek Chung

Cover Image: Bei Dao
Cover Design: Ann Mak

ISBN: 978-988-237-148-4

Published by The Chinese University of Hong Kong Press
The Chinese University of Hong Kong
Sha Tin, N.T., Hong Kong
Fax: +852 2603 7355
Email: cup@cuhk.edu.hk
Website: www.chineseupress.com

Printed in Hong Kong

目錄 Contents

鍾國強
Derek Chung

Translated by Tammy Lai-Ming Ho

水井

那是老家瞪向天空的一隻眼睛
我親眼看見工人把泥從裡面掏出來
濕濕黃黃，黏黏纏纏，然後便有了水
從地層深處源源滲出，瞬間浸滿了
眼眶。我把木桶垂下，一把回聲
恍若恍若，迴旋著漣淪一圈一圈
向聚散的游雲，說另一世界的話

那是桌上一杯水，靜止，陰沉
玻璃杯沿像井口的圍欄，我趨前
呼出的氣息轆轤而下，貼著苔綠的內壁
停在影子幢幢的水面。周遭沒有一絲風
但我感到水的清冷，沿我的內壁源源滲下
於是透明，看見底層微微挪動的物質

我在支流裡停止，兩旁新舊的樓房在蹲看
一輛巴士夾在前面的路口，交警的白手套揮舞
在黑壓壓蓄勢翻湧的頭顱之上，像無人注意的一絲浪花
身邊的人向天張大了口，沒有聲音，沒有手勢
文字像遠年的苔蘚，滲出古綠的顏色。我閱讀著
這城市的內壁，滑到最深最深的地方，又從那裡緩緩攀升

河水流動。壩下的水捲起了漩渦。黑色的水有白色的泡沫
我們在石上蹲著，用鎚子，有節奏地鎚打枯枝似的魚藤
滲出奶白色的汁液，流進底下錚錚錝錝的繁響裡
於是在堤岸不遠，我們看見仰向天空的魚肚白
像浮沉著的陰雲，偶然兩邊翻動，展示著死亡和希望

我們擠過了瓶頸，三股支流匯成一道大河
有人用擴音器捕獵憤怒，有人在計算收成
有人張大了口，發出別人的聲音
河水越流越洶湧，陽光猛烈
直射河的最底層，沉著已久的淤泥和污砂
翻湧上升，邊緣閃著耀眼的光芒

我把一尾尾暈眩的魚撈起，放進河灘上的草簍
有些魚擱淺在石上，在草桿間掙扎翻身
我看著那些翕動的嘴巴，彷彿聽到牠們的聲音
在輪迴吐放的一個一個泡沫裡。我把一尾活像喝醉的魚
隔開，放進一隻盛著清水的小木桶裡
看牠勉力將肚子翻過來，如翻動一塊古遠的泥磚
一座搖搖欲墜的房子，一個被撂下的行囊

回家吃過鮮美的魚粥，吐著細細的
骨刺，便見牠在小木桶裡悠悠醒轉

河水流到下游，又迂迴分叉湧向四面八方的淺灘
有人傲立河岸，像口號不斷升高，在幢幢商廈間不斷迴響
天空在窗洞裡默觀，堤壩在聲音裡顫抖，泡沫在爆破
我看到聲音，看到聲音裡面巨大的沉默，如一張一張魚的嘴巴

我想把魚放回河裡，但河裡也不是美好的所在
我想把魚放進瓦煲裡，但我們吃魚還不夠嗎？

河水的聲音在身後響起，在身邊響起，在身前響起
蓋過草桿旁的漪淪，石隙間的呼息，泥巴上的鱗屑
簍筐裡的血絲。當河水染成氣球，岸上便有人宣告
聽，請聽，請聽河裡一把碩大無朋涵蓋一切的聲音

我雙手把魚捧到井口，向著一個深邃的影子
放下，然後靜靜聆聽，遠遠，一個，只屬於那魚的，回聲

我們都在發出聲音嗎？誰在聆聽？一道偉大行進的河
浩浩蕩蕩，沖激著堤岸，發出水井永遠發不出的聲音

我想像那魚，在老房子旁的水井裡，孤獨地轉悠身體
彷彿一隻鱗閃的眼睛，瞪著魚肚白的天空

2003 年 7 月 17 日

The Well

It's the old home's eye glaring at the sky
My own eyes see workers scooping out mud
Wet, yellow, sticky and tangled, then the water comes
Oozing from the deep earth, in an instant soaking
The eye's rim. I lower the wood bucket, and an echo
Speaks—as though, as though, circling round and round—
Another world's language to the passing clouds that gather
    and disperse

It's a glass of water on the table, still, gloomy
Its rim is like the well's fence, and I lean forward
My breath going down the windlass, sticking to the moss-
    green inner walls
And resting on the water where shadows flicker. Everywhere
    is windless
Yet I feel the chill of the water seep down my insides
So translucent, the substances below are seen to slightly wriggle

I stop at a tributary, old and new buildings squatting and
    watching from both sides

A bus stuck at the junction ahead, the traffic officer's white
gloves waving
On a dark and surging skull, like an unnoticed ripple
Those beside me open their mouths to the sky, no voice,
no gestures
Writing like moss from years ago, leaking ancient green. I read
The inner walls of this city, slide to its deepest place, then
unhurriedly climb up

The river flows. The water below the dam rolls into whirls.
Black water makes white foam
We squat on rocks, rhythmically hammering jewelvine like
dead branches
The liquid oozing out is milky, and joins the complicated
sounds beneath
Not far from the embankment, where white fish maw faces
the sky
Like the dark clouds drifting along, its two sides
occasionally stirring, revealing death and hope

We squeeze through the bottleneck, three tributaries
converging into one great river
Someone hunts wrath with a loudspeaker, someone counts his
harvest
Someone opens his mouth wide, and the voice is that of another
The river surges up, fierce sunlight
Directly reaching the river's lowest part, long sedimented
sludge and filth
Rolling and rising up, edges shining bright

I dredge up the dizzy fish one by one, putting them in reed
baskets on the beach
Some are stranded on the rocks, some struggle to turn over
between grass stalks
I watch their mouths open and close, as if I could hear their voices
In the reincarnated bubbles. I separate one drunk-looking fish
From the others, placing it in a small wood bucket full of clear water
I watch it try to flip onto its stomach like turning an ancient brick
A crumbling house, a left-behind travel bag
Eating fresh fish congee at home, spitting out tiny
Bones, I see the fish languidly wake up, turning in the bucket

Downstream, the river divides circuitously into shallows that
  lead in all directions
Someone stands proudly on the riverbank, rising like a
  slogan echoing endlessly among office buildings
The sky observes window gaps in silence, dams tremble in
  sounds, bubbles burst
I see sounds, and see vast reticence in sounds, like the
  mouths of fish

I want to return the fish to the river, but the river is no fine place
I want to cook it in the clay pot, but have we not eaten enough fish?

The sounds of the river ring behind me, beside me,
  before me,
Overwhelming the ripples by the grass, the breaths in stone
  cracks, the scales on the mud
The wisps of blood in the basket. When the river is dyed
  balloons, someone on the shore will announce
Listen, please listen, listen to the river's thunderous sound, it
  encompasses everything

I cup the fish to the mouth of the well, toward a deep shadow
Put it in, and listen silently, as far away, the echo—the only
echo—of one solitary fish

Are we all making sounds like that? Who is listening? A
great river in motion
Majestic, crashing into embankments, creates a sound that
wells could never make

And I imagine that fish, turning alone in the well by the
old house
like a glistening eye, glaring at the sky as white as fish maw

17 July 2013

1：99

當我是1，你是99

當我把稀釋的漂白水倒進浴室的U型去水位
當我第23次用酒精紙巾揩抹雙手
當我嘗試再用點力，擦掉杯沿咖啡或茶的陳跡
今早，床腳下的灰，有一張收據

而幼腳蜘蛛大模大樣爬進相架背後露出便便大腹
給昨夜弄疲了的蜻蜓在光管下仰臥
我在網上第129次重看關於自己的信息
化名嘲諷，攻擊，然後矢口否認
自己是另一個自己很快便忘記的名字

當我拉開戴久了的口罩嗅到一股噁心的氣味
當我打開房子的頂蓋，警告上面一個也不認識的鄰居
當我開始學懂在骨碌碌的眼球中辨識新的符號
今早，電梯門打開，人群匆匆向兩邊的空氣稀釋

而一聲咳嗽可以免費換取身邊偌大的空間
維園一株樹木獨對躲開了的玻璃森林
我走過的路給自來水猛烈攻擊，電梯扶手

迎接盡頭塑料手套一團一團濡濡濕濕
圖書館緊急疏散前，我被一列一列靈魂拒絕

當我攤開地圖發現走過的地方從未走過
當我遮蓋眉眼露出下半臉的白色口罩
今早，當我揭開報章找尋醫院的新鮮數字
一隻僵固的蜉蝣正把蜘蛛驅逐出游絲

而我不敢開窗只得翻檢儲物櫃和抽屜
發現小津的秋刀魚塵封在希治閣的後窗
我問我們的結婚錄像要不要轉成光碟
你說你高聲地說誰看呢誰還看呢我說
甚麼甚麼隔著門廊走道隔著那麼多東西

當我用稀釋的漂白水洗過我們走過的地方
當我第221次用酒精抹盡所有扶手
當我取出萬能膠，嘗試黏回暴雨後霉脫的牆紙
今早，過期月結單內，有蟑螂乾屍

當你是1，而我是99

2003年10月10日

1:99

When I am 1, you are 99

When I pour diluted bleach down a U-bend
When I clean my hands with alcohol wipes for the 23rd time
When I try applying a little more force to wipe away the stains of coffee or tea from the rim
This morning, dust on the bed foot, there was a receipt

A thin-legged spider climbs pompously into the back of the photo frame showing its enlarged abdomen
Exhausted from last night, the dragonfly rests under the fluorescents
For the 129th time I re-read the news about me on the internet
By posters using pseudonyms to ridicule, attack, and then deny
I am another name that is quickly forgotten

When I remove my long-worn mask the odour is nauseous
When I open up my ceiling, I warn my upstairs neighbour, whom I do not know
When my rolling eyes learn to read new signs

This morning, the lift opened, the crowd rushed in
various directions, diluting the air

But a cough can get you the vast space around you for free
A single tree in Victoria Park faces a hiding forest of glass
The roads I've walked attacked by tap water, escalator handles
Are met with plastic gloves, clump after clump of wetness
Before the emergency evacuation at the library, I was
rejected by rows of spirits

When I spread out the map I discover I've never been to
those places that I've been to
When I cover up my eyebrows and eyes I expose my white
facemask beneath
This morning, when I opened the newspapers looking for
the hospital's new numbers
A stiff mayfly expelled a spider from its web

But I don't dare open the windows, I double-check the
cabinets and drawers

I find Otaru's mackerels covered in dust in Hitchcock's
rear window
I ask should we transfer our wedding tape to DVD
You say you loudly say who'll watch it who does still
watch it I say
What I say what separates the porch and the corridor it's
so many things

When I wash the places we went to with diluted bleach
When I clean all the handrails with alcohol wipes for the
221st time
When I took out the all-purpose paste, to glue back the
mouldy wallpaper loose from the storm
This morning, there were dried-out cockroach corpses
among the overdue monthly bills

When you are 1, and I am 99

10 October 2003

蝴蝶

深夜回來
關門
便看見了
你
我背後的
影子
不斷拍
翼

該讓你
進來
麼？
手停在
門把上
一
秒

你在
門檻上
徘徊

拍打著
失神的
燈

一秒

便平靜地
把你
寄入門縫

脫下
疲憊的
鞋
停止想念

遠方的人
或是我自己

2004年11月18日

The Butterfly

Returning home late
Closing the door
And seeing
You
Behind me
A shadow
Fluttering
Its wings

Should I
Let you
In?
A hand stays
On the doorknob
One
Second

You
On the doorsill
Wandering

Flapping
A distracted
Lamp

One second

Then silently
You are
Sent through the doorcrack

Taking off
Exhausted
Shoes
I stop missing

A faraway person
Perhaps it is me

18 November 2004

華田

我們讓光進去的時候
便發現裡面的粉末都凝結了
一塊塊像田裡翻出的泥團
我們用小匙敲鑿，它們退到罐緣
像一切從泥土裡出來的
那樣固執，不肯輕易粉碎

就像回家路上看見一桿鋤頭
在一望無人的田畦上靜止
崩缺的刃邊仍附著二三泥塊
默然等待下午茶後的勞動
背後總是筆直悠長的畦壟
給拌和的陽光，如昨日飽滿

如今穿過有如隧道的樹林
便見高速公路突兀在眼前
腰斬了的田堵住沒出路的水
還要拌合一種甚麼滋味呢？
營營蚊蚋中一座破廟
隱隱升起麻雀劈啪的鳴響

就像鬧市中我們不斷讓塵土
與砂粒依附，磨出心中越來越厚的
疙瘩，並恆常關在金屬華采中
讓情感乾掉。而在隆隆催趕聲中
我們總會不期然繞到商場背後
那些潮濡，卑微，晦暗的所在

我們讓光進來的時候
便發現我們都凝結了
一塊塊像田裡翻出的泥團
城市用目光敲鑿，我們退到邊緣
像一切從泥土裡出來的
那樣固執，不肯輕易粉碎

2008 年 8 月 12 日

Ovaltine

When we let the light in
We discover this powder has caked
Lumps like upturned mud in a field
Tapping the canister with a small spoon, the lumps return
to the edge
Like everything that comes out of soil
Obstinate, not easily crushed

Like seeing on the way home a hoe
Standing stock still in a small deserted field
The chipped blade edge retaining two or three clumps of mud
Silently waiting for work after tea
Behind it is always the straight and long field ridge
Lending yesterday's vigour to the evenly-blended sunlight

Now going through the tunnel-like forest
The highway appears abruptly before us
The cut-off field stops the trapped water
What kind of feeling should we mix together?
Within the swarm of mosquitoes is a broken temple
Faintly the loud clatter of sparrows rises

The way we continue to let dust and sand adhere
in a buzzing city, and grind into that thickening
Lump in our hearts, forever locked in the glory of metal
Emotions dry up. And in the rumbling, urging sounds
We always unconsciously go behind the backs of malls
Those wet, low, dark locales

When we let the light in
We find we are caked
Lumps like upturned mud in a field
The city taps us with its gaze, and we retreat to the edge
Like everything that comes out of soil
Obstinate, not easily crushed

12 August 2008

傍晚在鰂魚涌

——仿〈中午在鰂魚涌〉向也斯致意

這時我走到人群裡
太多人走在同一方向
從地底走出來
許多年前的記認好像刷落了
面前升起的是另一道天橋
街燈輸送寒氣
店面寫著生滾的粥
有人拿起煲仔飯進入裡面不見
有人看著玻璃
是凝固的街景還是自己

這時只是情緒
拖著白天的疑問拐進暗巷
有人耐心地摺疊一塊紙皮
有人呆望柱上劏開的空間
我在燈號前停下看燈
學習如實就在那裡
學習樓叢間的夜空
不敢輕言寬大

七重天的食客都寥落了
花檔還有人剪花
亂墜的枝葉與陳言
腳下傳來反覆的細響
老人用化學毛筆
顫顫描摹著千古
千朵花有千種顏色
密封在張掛的字詞裡

這時望向馬路
看見對面有人看我
這時望向商廈的玻璃
寬敞的大堂有朱銘在耍太極
電車空出來的窗
讓沿街某些風景穿過
偪仄的招牌
偶然出現幾個錯字
爐灶釋出善意的蒸氣
仍抹不掉鏡面的鏽跡
叮叮有時是警號

冒失的人回身大罵
有時只是寂寞
像寒夜裡觸手的雨滴
暖意一度停駐
又再開行

這時從殯儀館走出來
還好像擠在迴轉的梯間
千種人有千種心思
剪花人在擺脱剪影
執念在人面的河流中
前行還是後退
我走到地底的人群裡
學習像一列地車
沒有兩旁的風景
在金屬的聲音中認識人
不僅僅是自己的回聲

2013 年 1 月 14 日晚弔祭後作

Dusk at Quarry Bay

—After "Quarry Bay in the Afternoon,"
in honour of Leung Ping-kwan

This moment I am walking into a crowd
Too many are walking in the same direction
Emerging from underground
Marks from years ago seem to have been brushed off
In front of me rises one more overpass
Streetlamps transmit cold air
In a shop advertising congee raw or boiled
Someone carrying claypot rice disappears
Someone looks at the glass
The frozen street scene or himself

This moment is only a mood
Dragging daylight's limping doubts into dark alleys
Someone patiently folds a cardboard box
Someone blankly stares at the spaces columns cut open
I stop in front of the traffic lights looking at the lights
Learning that the facts are there
Learning that the night sky between dense buildings
Dare not speak lightly or be lenient

Diners in the Seventh Heaven Restaurant are sparse
Someone's still cutting flowers in the stall
A deluge of fallen branches, leaves and old speeches
Fine sounds repeat from beneath your feet
Old men use synthetic calligraphy brushes
Tremblingly tracing over words from ancient antiquity
One thousand flowers one thousand colours
Sealed in hanging texts

This moment I look at the road
And see someone looking back at me on the other side
This moment I gaze at the glass windows on office buildings
Ju Ming practises t'ai chi in a spacious lobby
Those empty windows on trams
Let the street scenes pass through
Packed shop signs
With occasional typos
Stoves emit benevolent steam
I can't rub off the rust on mirrors
Sometimes *ding ding* is an alarm
Reckless people turn around and swear

Sometimes it's just loneliness
Like raindrops touching hands on a cold night
Warmth stays for a time
Then leaves

This moment I walk out of a funeral parlour
Squeezed as if in a revolving stair
One thousand people one thousand thoughts
The flower cutter shredding silhouettes
Clinging to the river of faces
Moving forward or back
I enter the underground crowd
Learning to be like a train
Without scenery on either side
To learn about people through a metallic voice
Not only my own echo

Written after his memorial service on 14 January 2013

抽屜

那是一方僅容肉身的抽屜
從來沒有長大，從不陷進泥土
也毋需澆水；白天他穿梭於街巷
從瞎忙著的人群背後欠身而過
晚上拖著像掏空了的軀幹回去
插進一個亮著霓燈的，油膩的
把陰深的廊道完全敞開的裸身

他進出辦公室，商場，後巷和公廁
把一疊凌亂的A4紙抖開又閉合
沒有人看見內容，支票和輔幣
自動轉賬往他滿是刻痕的內壁
醫生從中摘掉三道疤，四顆瘜肉
銀行取回曾經承諾的數字，舊情人
刮去所有紀念日的紋身，和風景

沒有風景，便是閉合的，光潔的靈魂
他試圖擱在沙灘，斜靠在露天咖啡座
在戲院內遮擋別人的視線，在一樓一
讓年華還未完全老去的鳳姐無從下手
他努力擠出無可無不可的笑容

忙於吃，喝，排出一整族壁虎的乾屍
和依然保持體溫的，鮮軟的蟑螂卵

他瞪著肚臍的匙孔想像不曾有過的鑰匙
他試圖坦白，別人卻往他的身上丟零錢
試圖隱藏，埋在門牌的亂崗如失憶的墓碑
直至發覺自己忽然插不進昨夜的廊道
頹然跌進大街，剛好給一輛貨櫃車輾過
並來得及讓螢紅的尾燈照見甚麼也沒有的
木質，展現一截一截仿如人體的肌理

2012年9月12日

The Drawer

It's a drawer that only holds flesh
It never grows, or sinks into soil
It needs no watering; during the day he passes through streets
  and alleys
Walking behind the purposelessly preoccupied crowd
At night he drags his emptied-out body back
And plugs it into a lit neon lamp, greasily
Opening his complete nakedness to the deep dark corridor

He walks in and out of offices, malls, back lanes and public toilets
Shaking out and closing a pile of disarrayed A 4 paper
No one sees their content, the cheques and coins
Transfer automatically to his scar-covered wall
The doctor pulls down three scabs and four adenomatous polyps
The bank retrieves the once promised figures, former lovers
Scrape off all their memorial tattoos and scenery

No scenery, only closed, cleansed souls
He tries to stand on the beach, recline in an open-air café
Block another's line of sight in the cinema, in a one-woman brothel

The hooker hanging onto the last of her youth can't lay her hands
on him
He tries hard to squeeze out smiles that are neither here nor there
And busies himself eating, drinking, discharging a whole race of
gecko corpses
And still warm, fresh and soft cockroach eggs

He stares at the keyhole on his stomach imagining a key that was
never there
He attempts to be honest, but others throw coins at him
Attempts to hide the disorderly mound buried in his door plate
like an amnesiac tombstone
Until he notices he can no longer fit into last night's corridor
Disappointed, he falls in the street, where a truck runs him over
Just in time for the glowing red tail lights to shine on nothing
The wood displaying sections of body-like texture

12 September 2012

開在馬路上的雨傘

——詩援雨傘運動

開在馬路上的雨傘
不等雨也不等風
承著腳步那麼多天了
只有瀝青可退

開在馬路上的雨傘
綻開了石壆邊的兩片葉
夜涼了腳踝縮回營帳
天末一燈如豆仍黃

開在馬路上的雨傘
是尾站的空巴士
給遺忘了的一些甚麼
角落的黑，沒有一聲呼喊

開在馬路上的雨傘
沒有像傘一樣合上
開在雨傘上的馬路
也沒有像路一樣好走

2014年11月18日

Umbrellas Open on the Roads

—A poem in support of the Umbrella Movement

Umbrellas open on the roads
Waiting neither for rain nor wind
Bearing footsteps for so many days
Only asphalt can move them back

Umbrellas open on the roads
Two leaves bloom on the kerb
Cold nights, ankles retreating into tents
A bean-like light at day's end, still yellow

Umbrellas open on the roads
An empty bus's final stop
Give what has been forgotten
Darkness in the corner, without a sound of shouting

Umbrellas open on the roads
Not closing up like umbrellas
To forge a road on open umbrellas
Is not as easy as walking down the road

18 November 2014

內核的形狀

——給母親

午陽移諸牆角的蟻路
藤根仍在影子裡盤結
記憶本無所謂有
都在看庭前將枯的樹
思想本無所謂無
都只剩下骨了
攙持靜脈似的一紙
把瘿瘤留在彼方陰影處
懷妊，破光，血流
一地啼聲中懸沉默一果
把時間與文字
慢慢皺成了內核的形狀

2015年9月1日

The Shape of a Fruit Pit

—For mother

Noonsun shifts to the ant path at the corner of the wall
The vines are still entangled in the shadows
Memory doesn't care about having
It's in watching the tree in the front yard wither
Thinking doesn't care about having
Only bones remain
Supporting veins like paper
Leaving the tumour in the shades of elsewhere
Pregnant, worn out, blood flowing
Silence's fruit hangs in the land of howls
Slowly wrinkling time and word
Into the shape of its pit

1 September 2015

雨餘中一座明亮的房子

——向畢曉普（Elizabeth Bishop）的六節詩致敬

雷聲最響的時候也沒有驚動樹上的黃皮
雨水溜過一顆一顆，在末端凝聚重量
然後在失神的一刻倏然墜落，好像日子
逐一碎散。母親抬頭，還是聽不到任何聲音
偶然提起右手，顫顫指劃眼前的房子
像要在早前歷歷的怖慄中，重塑一個夢

母親那時仍堅持說，床邊的黑衣人絕不是夢
蝙蝠即使顛倒了日夜，黃皮依然是黃皮
她要提防纍纍的記憶逐一遠離房子
於是為菜肴下更多的鹽，為碗碟添加重量
不斷往返園門，撿回碎石與落葉的聲音
鎖起來，像月曆上，一個一個圈著的日子

父親又再重述，母親年輕時待在家鄉的日子
柴在灶裡，棺在樑上，糙米蒸出夾縫中的夢
那時母親剛學曉寫姓名，來信，須旁人讀出聲音
然後滯留廣州，蟬鳴過後，樹上還是酸澀的黃皮
抓一把泥，雨水中也不知增添多少重量
然後是磚牆，古得發綠，孤獨也像家鄉的土房子

如今這裡的十三呎半，也層層疊疊得有若那房子
田地在下，禽畜在中，根與血相連的那些日子
疊加一桌桌菜肴與狼藉，以及人散後空桌的重量
「去，去，去！」父親偶然也轉述母親的開口夢
然後給雷聲隱去，樹上是連飢鳥也不再吃的黃皮
在雨水中，諦聽園門內外，也只有雨水的聲音

母親回來的時候，像沒有回來般不發任何聲音
水井的漣淪也沒動，雨痂也沒有走進房子
然後電飯煲按了掣，蒜出香，箕側翻出一顆黃皮
然後是沒有剝離的咀嚼，連皮帶肉的日子
然後是清水，渠溝，碗歸碗碟歸碟，一床無夢
離去的步履也像回來，沒有增添更多重量

雷聲最響的時候天空有沒有一定的重量
打在人間？抽屜突然打開了，沒有聲音
照片冊也打開了，人工的描色褪回黑白的夢
一襲一襲都是黑衣人，穿過衣櫃，揹起房子
揹起那些不易走過也已走過的日子
走遠，成一道灰色的山線，淡去，一如黃皮

「帶回去吧。」夢中母親捧出剛摘的飽滿的黃皮
　　聲音中有雨水的味道，風雷光影交相鬱積的
　　日子
是要繼續承載那重量嗎？雨餘中一座明亮的房子

2016年2月20日

A Bright House After Rain

—In honour of Elizabeth Bishop's "Sestina"

The loudest thunder cannot shake the tree's wampees
Rain passes through them one after another, endpoints
  gathering weight
To suddenly fall at a distracted moment, like days
Shattered one by one. Mother looks up, hearing no sound
By chance raising her right hand, and points tremblingly at
  the house
As though from former terror she reinvents a dream

Mother insists the bedside man dressed in black is not a dream
Even if bats reverse day and night, wampees stay wampees
She guards against accumulated memories leaving the house
So adds more salt to the food, and to the plates more weight
Constantly returning to the garden gate, she picks up stone
  and leaf sounds
To lock them up like a calendar's circled days

Father once again recounts how, when young, Mother kept
  to her village days
Firewood in the stove, coffins on the beams, brown rice
  steaming crevice dreams

Mother had just learnt to write her name, still needed
someone to make her letters sounds
Then she was delayed in Guangzhou, after the cicadas
sang, on the tree still bitter wampees
Grab some mud, who knows how much the rain has
added weight
Then brick walls, so ancient they're green, as lonesome as
a village earthen house

Now these thirteen and a half square feet, stacked up like
that house
Field on the ground floor, poultry in the middle, roots
and blood linked in those days
Disorderly dishes piled up; people dispersing after meals,
leaving behind the empty tables' weight
"Go, go, go!" Sometimes Father relays mother's words in
her dreams
Drowned out by thunder, even hungry birds on the tree
won't eat those wampees
In the rain, listening carefully in and out of the garden,
only rain sounds

When Mother returns, as though she had never returned—
there's no sound
The ripples in the well don't stir, rain scabs don't enter the
house
The rice cooker's on, the scent of garlic, in the winnow
basket is a wampee
Chewing it without peeling off its skin, skin and flesh were
one in those days
Then clear water, gutter, bowls returning to bowls, plates to
plates, a bed without dreams
Footsteps of departure like those of returning, no added
weight

When the thunder is loudest does the sky add any weight
To this world? The drawer is suddenly open, no sounds
The photo album is open, the artificial colouring fades into
black and white dreams
All dressed in black going through the closet and carrying
the house
Carrying those difficult bygone days
Walking far, forming a grey mountain line, fading like a wampee

"Take these home." Mother in the dream takes out
the just-plucked plump wampees
Her sound tastes of rain; wind, thunder, light, and
shadows interweave on stagnant days
Do I continue to bear the weight? After the rain, a
bright house

20 February 2016

頑石

遇石
你以為頑
繞過它
回頭
你便是石
以為頑
繞過自己

2016 年 1 月 29 日

The Stubborn Rock

Encountering a rock
You think you have
Walked around it
Turning back
You are the rock
Thinking you have
Walked around yourself

29 January 2016

鍾國強（香港），香港大學文學院畢業。曾獲多屆香港中文文學雙年獎、青年文學獎、中文文學創作獎、香港藝術發展獎藝術家年獎（文學藝術）等獎項。著有詩集《圈定》、《路上風景》、《門窗風雨》、《城市浮游》、《生長的房子》、《只道尋常》、《開在馬路上的雨傘》、《雨餘中一座明亮的房子》，散文集《兩個城市》、《記憶有樹》、《字如初見》，小說集《有時或忘》，文學評論集《浮想漫讀》等。

Derek Chung (Hong Kong) graduated from the Faculty of Arts of the University of Hong Kong. His numerous accolades include Hong Kong Biennial Awards for Chinese Literature, Youth Literary Awards, Awards for Creative Writing in Chinese, as well as Artist of the Year (Literary Arts) of Hong Kong Arts Development Awards. He has published many poetry collections, including *Delineation*, *Scenery on the Road*, *Doors and Windows and Wind and Rain*, *Urban Plankton*, *A Growing House*, *Nothing Unusual*, *An Umbrella Opened on the Road*, and *A Bright House in Residual Rain*; essay collections *Two Cities*, *Trees in Memory*, and *Words at First Sight*; novel collection *Sometimes One May Forget*; as well as literary critique *Floating Thoughts, Unrestrained Reading.*

《沉默與言說》盒裝叢書
SPEECH AND SILENCE Box Set Collection

1 在耶路撒冷 **塔明・阿爾巴霍迪**
In Jerusalem **Tamim AL-BARGHOUTI**

2 裸體：激情研究 **安娜・露易莎・阿瑪拉爾**
Nude: A Study in Poignancy **Ana Luísa AMARAL**

3 抄寫員的自白 **馬克西姆・阿梅林**
The Scribe's Confession **Maxim AMELIN**

4 從道教到有神論 **雷納托・桑多瓦爾・巴希加盧波**
From Taoism to Teaism **Renato Sandoval BACIGALUPO**

5 絲詩 **簡・博文**
Silk Poems **Jen BERVIN**

6 沉默與血 **阿巴斯・貝東**
Silence and Blood **Abbas BEYDOUN**

7 論工人階級的卓越地位 **米若什・別德日茨基**
On the Preeminence of the Working Class **Miłosz BIEDRZYCKI**

8 詩人船 **安娜・布蘭迪亞娜**
Ship of Poets **Ana BLANDIANA**

9 傍晚在鰂魚涌 **鍾國強**
Dusk at Quarry Bay **Derek CHUNG**

10 縈魂之手 **路易絲・杜普蕾**
The Haunted Hand **Louise DUPRÉ**

11 可能 **弗羅斯特・甘德**
Beckoned **Forrest GANDER**

12 在寒山中 **黃有源**
On the Cold Mountain **HWANG Yu-Won**

13 那從庸常中升起的 **毛子**
Those that Rise from Mediocrity **MAOZI**

14 走進風景 **馬圖拉**
Entering the Landscape **MATHURA**

15 今天松尾芭蕉掌勺 **塞爾希奥・萊蒙迪**
Today Matsuo Bashō Cooks **Sergio RAIMONDI**